MENTORING LIKE JESUS

Making Discipleship a Part of Everyday Life

Brad Merchant

Warner Press, Inc.
Warner Press and "Warner Press" logo are trademarks of Warner Press, Inc.

Mentoring Like Jesus
Written by Brad Merchant

Warner Press Inc
2902 Enterprise Dr
P.O. Box 2499
Anderson, IN 46013

www.warnerpress.org

Editor: Karen Rhodes
Cover Design: Curtis Corzine
Layout Design: Katie Miller

ISBN: 9781593179847
Printed in USA

Introduction

The unknown scares me. When I was a young boy my parents put me in swimming lessons in hopes of me becoming the next Michael Phelps (in case you were wondering, it never happened). The idea of swimming lessons sounded like a great idea at first until I realized something: I had to swim in the deep end. I still remember the day when the swim instructor was floating in the deep end of the pool with his arms out for me to jump to him. Somehow, I managed to jump with buckling knees and teary eyes! Why was I so scared? Because I was worried I would drown or not remember all the techniques you need to stay afloat. I was afraid the instructor would let me slip into the abyss of the pool. I was afraid of the unknown. I am still afraid of the unknown.

The thought of flying still scares me because I'm always thinking, *will we crash? Will this plane operate like it's supposed to? Will I get on the right plane?* Perhaps you can relate. For all of us, there is something that can spur us on to be anxious and fearful because there is an unknown element to it.

It is this fearful and anxiety-producing, unknown reality that I believe holds back many Christians from biblical discipleship and mentoring.

Like a child scared to jump into a pool, many Christians never make disciples simply because they aren't sure what to do and they don't want to fail.

That is why I've written this book. My aim is to help Christians make discipleship a part of everyday life by sharing practical steps on why and how to do that. My hope is that while reading this book "the eyes of your heart may be enlightened" (Ephesians 1:18 NIV) so you would see discipleship and mentoring as an indispensable calling of the Christian life.

So here is the question: If discipleship is an indispensable calling of the Christian life, then what exactly *is* discipleship?

What is Discipleship?

In his book titled *Discipling: How to Help Others Follow Jesus*, Mark Dever defines discipleship as "Helping others follow Jesus."[1]

Chuck Lawless defines discipleship in his book, *Making Disciples Through Mentoring* as "A God-given relationship in which one growing Christian encourages and equips another believer to reach his/her potential as a disciple of Christ."[2]

After thinking on these definitions and the overall teaching of the Bible on discipleship, I would define discipleship in this way: one Christian helping another Christian to grow in Christ.

Christian discipleship is centered in the giving of one's self for the spiritual benefit of another.[3] To disciple is to pick up your cross, die to self, (Luke 9:23) and help another Christian grow in Christ.

Still, another question lingers. If discipleship is one Christian helping another Christian to grow in Christ, why is it important that we do it?

Why Discipleship?

The last recorded words of Jesus, better known as the Great Commission, are found in the Book of Matthew, 28th chapter. It's in these last words that we find the heartbeat of Christ and the very heartbeat He desires His people to have today. "Go therefore and make disciples of all nations, baptizing them in the name of the Father and of the Son and of the Holy Spirit, teaching them to observe all that I have commanded you. And behold, I am with you always, to the end of the age" (Matthew 28:19-20).

There are three aspects to this commission that Christ gives to His disciples.

The first is *Command*. Notice this was not a request. Jesus did not say, "Hey guys, if you are up for it or feel gifted for the task, make disciples!" Instead, He says, "*Go* therefore and make disciples of all nations." This means that Christians, those who have placed their faith in Christ, are called to be disciple-makers as much as they are called to read their Bibles and pray. Discipleship is not a multiple-choice option for Christian obedience.

Christians either make disciples or disobey God. It's that simple.

Next is *Teaching*. After Jesus *states* what He is commanding, He then moves on to *explain* what He is commanding, "…make disciples of all nations, baptizing them in the name of the Father and of the Son and of the Holy Spirit, teaching them to observe all that I have commanded you."

Discipleship is more than just spending time with people. Discipleship involves teaching people about who God is and what He has done by modeling and proclaiming His Word. Discipleship without teaching is like a kite without wind. It doesn't function the way it ought to because it is missing the very thing that makes it work! Biblical discipleship always involves teaching or it ceases to be discipleship.

The last aspect of this commission is *Help*. God never calls His people to a task without providing His grace to accomplish the task. The Great Commission is no different.

After commanding His disciples and giving them instructions on how to follow through with the task, He leaves them with these words, "And behold, I am with you always, to the end of the age." It's as if He is saying, "I know this is a task that seems overwhelming, but remember this: I will *always* be with you."

What comfort the disciples must have found in those words! And what comfort we find in those words today as we look at this command to make disciples. You might feel unqualified, overwhelmed, and fearful at the thought of discipling others.

But hold on to this truth: God is with you and will help you accomplish the task. What confidence this gives us as we are assured that we will not be alone in this calling to make disciples!

Why disciple others? Because God has given His people the honor of building His kingdom! And the way God is building His everlasting kingdom is through discipleship.

What About Mentoring?

So how does discipleship apply to a book about mentoring? In what ways are they connected? Is it possible to make disciples and be a mentor at the same time? What is a mentor anyway?

From the Christian worldview, mentoring and discipleship are in many ways synonymous. You can't talk about discipleship without talking about mentoring and you can't talk about mentoring without talking about discipleship.

To grow and help others grow in Christ, the practice of mentoring must take place. You mentoring other Christians is a means God uses to "make disciples of all nations." The natural question we must ask in light of this is what exactly is mentoring?

What is Mentoring?

While the Bible doesn't answer this question directly, it certainly gives examples of what it looks like. The Apostle Paul exhorted Timothy to take all that he had learned from him and to "entrust to faithful men, who will be able to teach others also" (2 Timothy 2:2).

Paul encouraged Titus to challenge older women to teach and train the younger women in the church how to love their husbands and children, to be self-controlled, pure, and so forth (Titus 2:3-5). Jesus, in the pursuit of His mission to "seek and save the lost" (Luke 19:10), focused much of his time on mentoring His disciples. He spent time with His disciples (John 3:22), taught His disciples (Luke 11:1-13), and modeled what He wanted them to learn (John 13:15).

Repeatedly, the Bible contains examples of Christians teaching and training other Christians how to live out all that Jesus taught. This is precisely what it means to mentor.

To mentor is to intentionally train other people how to live, love, and glorify Christ. This is exactly what ties discipleship and mentoring together. They both are centered on giving your time and resources to help others know Jesus more.

What does this mean for you and me? It means that if we are to fulfill the Great Commission, we must be people who mentor. We must intentionally teach others all that Jesus commanded so that we might see Gospel advancement throughout all the world. This is our aim (Mark 16:15).

Mentoring is not a pursuit to grow your influence and teach people everything you know. Mentoring is a pursuit to see Jesus glorified in the lives of the people in whom you invest.

A Personal Story

When I look at the landscape of my life one thing is evident: God has used people to shape me into the person I am today—God uses His people to shape us into His image. Whoever walks with the wise becomes wise (Proverbs 13:20). Wisdom has a way of rubbing off on those who intentionally brush themselves up against it.

Practically speaking, wise people are those who surround themselves with wise people. They listen to them. Watch them. Learn from them. And in doing so, they themselves become more like them.

This is precisely God's plan for growing us into Christ's image. David Powlison put it best when he wrote, "Godly growth is most frequently mediated through the gifts and graces of brothers and sisters in Christ."[2]

Of all the stories I could share that prove this to be true, the story I know best is my own. When I was 17 years old I began to ask questions I had never considered before. Questions like, "What is the meaning of life? What do I want my life to amount to? Who is God?" Soon after, God used a young man to proclaim the Gospel to me. After hearing that Jesus lived the life I couldn't, died the death I should have, and rose again to forgive my sin, I placed my faith in Christ and became a "new creation" (2 Corinthians 5:17). Not long after my conversion, I sensed a desire for pastoral ministry. I wanted to proclaim this message of forgiveness to the world. I wanted people to experience Jesus the way I had experienced Him—I wanted to be a pastor.

Two years later God opened a door for me to become a pastoral intern at a church where I would later be ordained into Gospel ministry, meet lifelong friends, and eventually marry my wife. It was in this church that God allowed me to meet a man who would impact my life in innumerable ways.

I first met him in a Bible study and immediately was drawn by his passion to know God. It was apparent by the way he led his family, lived his life, and served others that he was serious about the Gospel. This brings up an important point: if you want to mentor others, don't start by broadcasting it to the world. Start by "walk[ing] in a manner worthy of the gospel" (Philippians 1:27). Love Jesus, serve people, and others will take notice.

I invited this man to meet with me at a local coffee shop one Tuesday morning. Little did I know we would end up meeting at that same coffee shop, at the same time, every Tuesday for the next two years. We discussed an array of things—theology, sports, family, church, personal struggles, frustrations, joys, and so much more—we shared life together. Looking back, I realize some of the most transformative times of my life came from conversations with this man on Tuesday mornings. Why? Because this man did four things all effective mentors do:

1. He pursued me. He set up meetings with me, contacted me outside of our regular meeting times, and wanted me to know that I was important to him.

2. He asked me the hard questions. He never shied away from asking me questions that would cause me to examine the state of my soul. Questions like, "In what ways have you failed this week? How is your marriage? What is the most frustrating thing in your life right now?" Great mentors ask the tough questions.

3. He was my friend. This is important. If the person you are mentoring feels more like a project than

a partner in growth, he will inevitably withhold vulnerability. My mentor invited me into his life. We went out to lunch and watched sporting events together. He became a great friend while being a great a mentor.

4. He passionately pursued holiness. The greatest gift you can give those you are leading is your personal example of living for Christ. When I saw my mentor pursue the Lord, his wife, his children, and those around him with passion and love, I was challenged to do the same.

In his excellent book, The Mentoring Church, Phil Newton makes this point clear:

> "Mentors must never minimize the power of example in shaping their (disciples). The way that they live out the Christian life, handle difficult conversations, maintain a healthy marriage, and love the body of Christ presses Christian character and practice for the disciple without ever conducting a class on it."[4]

Mentor, your holiness matters.

Now What?

It's clear that God desires for His people to make disciples and one of the main vehicles to do that is through mentoring. I'm convinced that many Christians understand this, but still don't mentor or disciple others—The reason being—they don't know how.

Perhaps you can relate. You want to mentor others. You want to intentionally train others with the Good News, hopefully, to see Gospel advancement in your church, community, and beyond. But, the problem is that you don't know how. You aren't sure where to start, what to say, who to mentor, and on and on it goes.

As you continue reading this book, I hope you will find practical wisdom on how to mentor others in everyday life. My desire is that after you read this book you will feel confident and empowered to make disciples through mentoring—accomplishing the Great Commission. So, sit down, grab a pen, and ask God to give you wisdom as you journey these pages and seek to become a better disciple of Jesus Christ!

Where Do I Start?

Years ago, I had my eyes opened to the realization that if we are Christians, we are called to make disciples. This realization sparked in me a desire to disciple others and see the Gospel go forth in my church, community, and the world. I had just one problem: I didn't know where to start.

Perhaps you find yourself in a familiar situation. You understand that to be a Christian is to be a disciple-maker, but you aren't sure how to go about it. You want God to use you to make a difference in the lives of people around you through mentoring, but starting has you at a standstill.

You're not alone. And thankfully, God, by His grace, has given us help in His all-sufficient Word to know how to get started in the kingdom-advancing work of discipleship.

As the Puritan, Thomas Watson once said, "He that commands us, will enable us." With that understanding, here are four things to do as you look to get started in the work of mentoring others for God's glory:

1. Pray.

Ask God to provide you with someone to mentor and to give you wisdom in showing you someone that you might already know who could be mentored. God loves to give wisdom to those who ask Him for it (James 1:5). It is through prayer that God will provide someone for you to mentor and grow in Christ with.

2. Look.

In my own life, I have found that God often provided me with someone to mentor that I already know—I just need to open my eyes. Ask yourself the question, "Who do I know that I could start meeting with to help them grow in Christ?" When you ask this question, you'll be able to think critically about the people God has *already* placed in your life. Who are you already "rubbing shoulders with" on a regular basis that you could pour your life into? Start asking and start looking.

3. Pursue.

When God reveals the one you could possibly mentor, pursue him or her. Don't wait for people to ask you to mentor them. I fear many disciples aren't made because many disciples aren't pursued. Set up a time to get together with them for coffee or a meal. I like to tell people that they need to "pursue people on to your calendar." In other words, pursue someone and get a date on your calendar to meet with him or her. Pursuing someone communicates to her that you care for her and want to give your time to investing in her.

4. Pray (again).

After you have met with a potential person to mentor, pray about what you should do next. Should you continue meeting with this person? Does this person have an interest in continuing to meet? Would this person be a valuable investment of your time? Ask yourself these questions and ask God to give you wisdom.

These are four easy steps you can take to get started in the process of mentoring. In doing these steps you will be able to gain clarity as to whom you will mentor and what that mentoring relationship will look like moving forward.

Building on the Foundation

There are a couple of principles to keep in mind— not rules to follow as much but wise guidelines that are helpful in any mentoring relationship. Here are three:

1. Mentoring isn't teaching people all you know.
I once heard Tim Keller say, "Bad evangelism says: I'm right, you're wrong, and I would love to tell you about it." In the same way, bad mentoring says: I know a lot, you don't, and I would love to teach you. We all have that person in our lives that acts like an all-knowing sage, just waiting to give you his all-wise counsel with any chance he gets. Mentoring does not work the way God intended it to work with people who act that way.

Proverbs 18:2 says, "A fool takes no pleasure in understanding, but only expressing his opinion." This means that if you are zealous about doing the work of discipling/mentoring simply because you want to teach someone everything you know, you don't understand mentoring. Mentoring is about caring for another person's soul with the intentional purpose of helping him grow in Christ. Focus on loving people, not simply using them as a platform to share everything you know.

2. Seek to do life with others.

Discipleship is organic in the sense that it can't necessarily be put on a time schedule. Instead, discipleship happens during ordinary and everyday life. This means that some of the most important conversations and moments you can have in a mentoring relationship happen in the context of ordinary moments. You are sharing coffee with someone and he shares about past hurt and failure. You are at a ball game with someone and he asks you how you handled a similar situation he is going through.

Often, I have found that my mentoring relationships are nurtured best by sharing life with the people I'm investing in. Open your home, share coffee, a meal, or go to an event with other people. It's in the context of those times that God often grows people into His image.

3. Crucify yourself.

This is an important, yet often overlooked, aspect of discipleship: dying to self. If your goal in discipleship is to feel good about yourself because of the many people you are discipling, but look down on others at the same time for how inactive they are, you've got it all wrong. Discipleship requires us coming to the Lord and asking Him to advance His Kingdom through the work of discipleship.

What does this mean practically? It means we seek to do spiritual good to others without expecting anything in return. We give our time, energy, and resources to other people, prayerfully expecting that God will use us in the lives of other people to help them grow in Christ. Are you willing to give your life to help others follow Jesus?

Use Your Bible

There are only three things you need to make disciples: You, the Holy Spirit, and your Bible. Yet how often does the Bible get neglected in this important work? If the Bible is truly inspired, inerrant, and sufficient (and it is! See 2 Timothy 3:16), then we dare not neglect it. Instead, we should focus our mentoring relationships on the Bible. We should use it as an instrument to direct our understanding of who God is and what He has called us to do because of what He has done. Here are a couple of practical ways to use the Bible in the everyday work of mentoring:

1. Read it together.

This might seem obvious, but are you doing it now in your discipling relationships? The probability isn't very high. Yet what could possibly be more profitable to those you are mentoring than to read the Bible with them? The Scriptures renew our minds (Romans 12:2), help us have the mind of Christ (1 Corinthians 2:16), and show us the glory of God in Christ (2 Corinthians 3:18). As the Princeton theologian B.B. Warfield once said, "The Bible is the Word of God in such a way that when the Bible speaks, God speaks." This means the Bible speaks with the same authority that Jesus Christ did in the flesh. Why not read the very words of God with those you are discipling?

2. Memorize it together.

Psalm 119:11 says, "I have stored up your word in my heart, that I might not sin against you." This teaches us that memorization of Scripture leads to mortification of sin. When we are storing up or treasuring God's Word in our hearts and minds, we are enabled to crucify the flesh and its desires (Galatians 5:24).

I once heard an older man tell me that he had been mentoring a younger man in his church for five years. On the first week of meeting with him, he committed to memorizing two verses of Scripture with the young man each week. After five years, they had memorized over 500 verses of Scripture! He told me that their relationship grew stronger as they held each other accountable to storing up God's Word in their hearts. Memorize the Bible with those you mentor and watch your relationship (and soul) flourish!

3. Pray it together.

My friend, Dr. Donald Whitney wrote a book entitled, *Praying the Bible* (Crossway, 2015) that teaches us that praying the Bible is one of the most effective and helpful ways to pray. Shortly after I read this book and heard Dr. Whitney teach on this topic, I began to implement praying the Bible in my discipling relationships. What began to happen was incredible.

As we would pray the Bible together week after week and month after month, I found that we began to grow together in not only our prayer lives, but also our knowledge of God. Because our prayers and our minds were Bible-saturated, we began to live and look more like Christ as a result. Perhaps you could set up a time to meet with someone to simply pray the Bible with him, to grow in your knowledge of God and His Word together!

4. Listen to it together.

One of the best ways you can grow in your knowledge of God and help others do the same is in the context of the local church. Hearing faithful, Gospel-driven preaching week after week with those you are mentoring is one of God's means of grace for transforming us into the image of His Son and building unity between like-minded believers.

One of the ways I have applied this in my life is by meeting with a man who mentors me on Tuesday mornings. We meet at a coffee shop and share what we thought about the Sunday sermon—sermons we had listened to that week, and what we were currently reading. This proved to be an enriching time as we encouraged one another in our pursuit of knowing God's Word. Listen to the Word of God with those you are discipling.

The Bible is a great gift to us. It is God's revelation to us concerning who He is, what He has done, and what He is doing. And He promises that when we commit ourselves to it and teach it to others, it will not return void (Isaiah 55:11). So let's use His Word in our discipling/mentoring relationships to further the Gospel and see many people conformed to the image of Christ!

Be Intentional

On a recent trip to a wedding with my wife, we began talking about a couple of things that had come up at work that day and the various things we needed to get done around our house. After some time went by and our conversation had ended, I realized we had driven past our exit miles back down the road! What happened? I wasn't intentional in looking for our exit. Because I wasn't intentional, I missed an opportunity to get to my destination the best and quickest way.

I fear we miss many opportunities to help others follow closer to Jesus, simply because we are not intentional. We miss making the most of ordinary moments and miss out on seeing those we are mentoring grow in Christ. This raises an urgent question we must answer: How are we to be intentional? Here are a few ideas:

1. Understand that time is a gift.

Moses prays in Psalm 90:12, "So teach us to number our days that we may get a heart of wisdom." Our days are numbered. God has, by His grace, given us time. Time that He intends us to use carefully, wisely, and intentionally. This means we must look at our schedule not as an instrument to serve self, but as a gracious gift to use for the glory of God. And what better way to bring Him glory with our time than to use it mentoring others!

2. Use your time in redemptive ways.

Paul writes in Ephesians 5:15-16, "Look carefully then how you walk…making a best use of the time." Because time is a gift, we must constantly seek to use it in redemptive ways. In other words, we should always be asking ourselves the question, "How can I use my time to advance the redemptive purposes of God?"

When we do this, we look at even *ordinary* moments differently because even *ordinary* moments can be used to advance Christ's mission. Driving in the car, running errands, or working around the house can all be redeemed when your time is viewed as something that can be used to serve redemptive purposes.

3. Don't waste your time.

Donald Whitney writes in his book *Spiritual Disciplines of the Christian Life,* "If people threw away their money as thoughtlessly as they throw away their time, we would think them insane. Yet time is infinitely more precious than money because money can't buy time." I often wonder how much time I waste that could be used intentionally to help others grow in Christ. How many times have I been physically present and mentally absent with someone I could encourage and grow with? Let's use God's gift of time intentionally and not waste it.

Books Are Your Friend

We live in a world today that is made up of more lookers than readers. What I mean by that is more people enjoy looking at something (television, social media, pictures, etc.) than reading something (books). David Wells put it well when he said; "The cultural mantle has passed from the users of words to the makers of images." Entertainment is easy, but reading takes work. Yet, it is a fruitful work—a work that is very helpful in the calling to mentor and make disciples. So how can you use books in your everyday calling to make disciples? Here are a few ideas:

1. Choose good books.
Every book has a voice. The question to ask when picking up a book is "what is this book saying?" If discipleship is one Christian helping another Christian to grow in Christ, we should be reading books that help us to that end. Find books that exalt Christ and proclaim the Gospel. Read them, give them away, and share what you learn from

them with others. Use good books that speak of the glories of the Gospel and accept nothing less.

2. Use books to delight in God.

I have found that good books, which share the glories of Christ, have helped me and those I'm discussing the book with find joy in Christ. Find a good book and share with your disciples what you are learning, encouraging them to enjoy a closer walk with Christ. God often uses books that are centered on Him to kindle in our hearts a greater delight in Him.

3. Read a book with someone.

It's simple, easy, and effective. Some of the greatest mentoring relationships are those that revolve around books. We read them together, discuss them together, and grow together by reading them with one another.

Prepare questions to discuss before you meet, based on the book you are reading together. Read others' thoughts on the book and discuss their viewpoints. Books are a great means God has given us to encourage one another in godliness. Pick up a couple, give one to a friend, and start to read it together to the glory of God!

Invite Others into Your Life

Mentoring is an intentional relationship that requires two things: teaching and modeling. As stated previously, discipleship without teaching ceases to be discipleship. However, discipleship that is void of modeling what is being taught ceases to be discipleship as well. The Apostle Paul told the church at Corinth to "Follow my example" (1 Corinthians 11:1 NIV) as he imitated Christ. Later, in the Book of Philippians, he told the church at Philippi to practice the things he had taught them and modeled (Philippians 4:9). In one of his last letters, Paul told Timothy to "practice these things" that Paul had taught him so that "all may see your progress" (1 Timothy 4:15).

For Paul, modeling what you have learned was just as important as teaching. At the end of the day, you will always be practicing your theology. If you believe you have been forgiven in Christ, you will function out of that belief and forgive those who sin against you (Ephesians 4:32). If you believe that God is sovereign over all things in your life, you will function out of that belief, and trust Him by faith even when you are in difficult circumstances (Psalm 13:5).

This means that one of the most effective means we have for mentoring others is our very lives. When we invite others into our lives to share life with us, we are allowing them to see us "walk in a manner worthy of the gospel" (Philippians 1:27). The impact this can have on another person's life is enormous. Gregory of Neocaesarea (A.D. 213-270) wrote about how his mentor and teacher Origen impacted him:

> He stimulated us by the acts he performed more than by the theories he taught…. Less obvious, but more important…was the fellowship with this man. Where I was blind he guided me. He taught me the truth concerning the Word. It was like a spark dropping into my inmost soul and catching fire there.[5] (Bruce Shelley, *Church History in Plain Language*).

What impacted Gregory the most was not Origen's teaching, writings, or sermons. What impacted him the most was the "fellowship with this man." How encouraging! You and I can have an impact on the lives of other people simply by inviting them to enter our lives and watch how we live.

This begs us to ask ourselves the question, "Am I inviting other people into my life to watch how I live?" I'm convinced that no matter how busy you are, you can do this! Here are a few ways that I try to invite others into my life:

1. Invite others to participate in tasks I have.
I have found that many of the people I am mentoring want to spend time with me regardless of the context. One of the ways I have attempted to redeem my time is by inviting those I'm mentoring to join me in completing tasks that I have to get done. This means that if I need to do some yard work, I'll invite a guy I'm mentoring to come and join me in it. This creates a relaxed environment where we can talk about God, life, and whatever is on our hearts.

Ask yourself this question: what do I need to get done this week that I could invite someone else to do with me? Whether its grocery shopping, taking the car into a mechanic, or working out, invite others to share life with you, allowing them to be shaped into Christ's image as they watch the way you live.

2. Share meals.

What I don't mean by this is that I split every meal I have with the people I am mentoring. What I do mean is that I rarely eat alone. Sharing meal times with people can be an effective way to have meaningful conversations about life and the Gospel. Jesus Himself was found eating with His disciples and even those that the world rejected throughout the New Testament Gospels. Why?

As Tim Chester says in his book, *A Meal with Jesus,* "Meals are a powerful expression of welcome and friendship in every culture." Meals are a pathway into the lives of people. Why not use your mealtimes to having meaningful conversations about life with those you are mentoring for the sake of the Gospel?

3. Enjoy life with other people.

I love basketball. I love to play it, watch it, talk it, and everything in between. So, one of the ways I have tried to incorporate mentoring and discipleship in every area of my life is by doing what I enjoy with other people! Recently, I took several men from my church to a professional basketball game to spend time together and enjoy watching the game. It proved to be a great encouragement and bonding experience among all of us as we laughed together, talked about what was on our hearts, and just enjoyed the time spent with one another.

What do you enjoy that you could invite someone else to join you? What hobby do you have that could be used by God to develop a deeper relationship with someone else? Invite others to participate in the things that you enjoy, and give God an opportunity to shape their hearts as they watch your life.

4. Serve together.
To date, the people I serve with are the closest friends I have. Serving is an avenue through which you grow in your affections toward God and your relationships with others. Ask yourself the question, "What are some ways that I can serve God and invite others along?"

Finding the Right Mentee

I love to see people develop and grow. It's invigorating to me, in part, because I realize that mentoring is a means God uses to fill the earth with "the knowledge of the glory of the Lᴏʀᴅ, as the waters cover the sea" (Habakkuk 2:14). But another motivating factor is joy. "I have no greater joy than to hear that my children are walking in the truth" (3 John 1:4). One of the greatest experiences of joy God can give is seeing God work through the people He has allowed you to mentor. It is this joyful experience, even in the midst of the sacrifice and work mentoring demands, that motivates me to keep investing in others.

One of these sources of joy for me was a young man we will call Bob. He has been an encouragement to me the three years I have known him. Our friendship began when we met for lunch to get to know one another. Discovering that we had similar interests, we began to spend more regular time together. Eventually, we met once a week for three years. We read books together, discussed ways we hoped to grow, and prayed with one another. At times we confronted one another, wept together, and often laughed with one another. We viewed our friendship as a great gift from God.

As we continued to meet, I began to see noticeable changes in Bob's life. He became more Christlike, he developed his love for the Bible, and a greater love for the church. He grew in humility. As time went on I began to see Christ formed in Bob (Galations 4:19). Soon, I saw things in Bob that I longed to see in myself! His eagerness to learn, grow, and develop as a Christ follower challenged me to learn, grow, and develop too. God was using our ordinary friendship to sharpen each other into the likeness of Christ (Proverbs 27:17). To this day, when Bob and I meet, I leave our time together encouraged to grow in my love for Christ and His people.

While my mentoring relationship with Bob is such a joy, I could also tell you stories of others I have attempted to mentor that were more of a burden. I have tried to invest in people that refuse to change, refuse to be vulnerable, and refuse to be passionate about the Gospel and God's glory. These stories are both frustrating and heartbreaking. Yet, if we are honest, we can all tend to be apathetic and hypocritical. Even Bob went through seasons where he seemed to droop into these valleys. So the question is this: what set Bob apart from the rest? Or in a broader sense, what qualities does a flourishing disciple have in a mentoring relationship? I believe there are three:

1. Humility.

Perhaps humility, more than any other characteristic, is most important. C.J. Mahaney defined humility well when he wrote, (Humility is) "honestly assessing ourselves in light of God's holiness and our sinfulness."[6] Humble disciples are flourishing disciples because they see themselves through the lens of the Gospel. A disciple that believes he has it all together will inevitably refuse counsel, reject correction, and resist any notion that he needs to learn. Mark it: the quickest way to stunt your growth as a Christian is to believe you are not a broken, needy sinner in need of others.

2. Curiosity.

In my experience, the most life-giving disciples I've mentored are those who are relentlessly curious. They love to ask questions because they love to learn. Curious disciples want to know the how, the what, and the why behind almost everything. Why? Because they desire to grow, change, and flourish as Christian disciples. Learning begins when we ask questions. Curiosity is the beginning of learning and growing.

3. Gratitude.

One of the greatest gifts a disciple can give his mentor is his gratitude. Bob lived this out more than any other person I've ever mentored. He frequently thanked me for meeting with him and investing in his life. I remember on several occasions getting thank you cards from him, expressing his gratitude for my mentoring. These acts of gratitude did two things for me. First, I felt affirmed and encouraged by Bob. His words and notes helped affirm that God was truly using me in his life. Second, my desire to invest in Bob grew tremendously. Because I knew God was using me in our relationship through Bob's intentional affirmation, I wanted to keep pouring my life into him. Gratitude is the key to a healthy mentoring relationship.

Your Home Is a Gift. Share It!

Several years ago I attended a mission's conference at a local church where a panel discussion of missionaries was taking place. I don't remember anything from that night except the last question asked. The question was directed toward a couple that had retired from decades of foreign mission work. The question was, what was your greatest tool for evangelism while on the mission field? Their answer? "Love and our home."

The answer surprised me. How could their home be one of the greatest tools for evangelism? They went on to explain how they realized that people feel welcomed, accepted, and loved when you invite them into your home and make them feel "at home." They saw several people converted in response to opening their home, building relationships with them, and sharing the Gospel through everyday conversations.

This begs us to ask the question, "How am I using my home?" If the home is a great tool for building relationships with people, why not use it to mentor and disciple others? Why not use God's gift to you (your home) and turn it into a gift to others (by loving and welcoming others into it)? A friend of mine caught hold of this vision and had an "open house night" every Friday night. Whoever wanted to come over was welcome between 5:00 and 11:00 PM, to hang out and spend time with him and his family. This proved to be a great blessing not only to those who came, but also to his entire family.

The point here isn't to have your home open on a certain day for an allotted amount of time each week. The point is to view your home as an opportunity to welcome people into your life and encourage them to grow in Christ. How can you use your home this week to serve the people of God and advance God's kingdom in your community?

Redeem Your Time at Church Gatherings

Church gatherings can become a lot like brushing your teeth if you're not careful. Every morning I get up, I walk to the bathroom and brush my teeth. I don't necessarily think about what I'm doing or how I'm going to do it, I just do it. It's routine. I've been brushing my teeth for so long now that I get ready without much thought, intention, or difficulty.

This is how many Christians function in church gatherings. They come and sit in the same place, talk to the same people, and leave as quickly as possible. We are all guilty of this. And when we choose to treat and view church gatherings in this way, we miss out on a great opportunity to pour into other people's lives. Here are a few ways to fight against the routine of just "coming" to church and, instead, intentionally disciple/mentor others in the context of church gatherings:

1. Walk in with a selfless heart attitude.

Church is not about you. It's about bringing God glory by gathering with the redeemed to bring Him praise. Tony Payne touches on this in his book, *How to Walk into Church,* when he writes:

> Church is not about me. It's not about the experience I have or what I get out of it. Church is a classic opportunity to love my brothers and sisters who are there, by seeking to build them up in Christ.[7]

When we walk into church each Lord's day, we should do so with a heart that is focused on bringing God praise and encouraging those around us. Without this heart attitude, it is impossible to be an instrument in God's hand to disciple others.

2. Encourage with spiritual conversations.

Go into your church gathering, seeking to encourage others. This is not a suggestion, but a command God gives all those who claim to be His (1 Thessalonians 5:11). How can we do this? By reminding others of who they are in Christ (Ephesians 1 and 2). By commending others for the grace of God at work in their lives (Hebrews 3:13). By using words that will build up a person and spur them on to godliness and good deeds (Hebrews 10:24). Seek to go into church gatherings with words of encouragement, rather than discouragement on your tongue.

3. Look for opportunities to meet new people.

How often do we come into church gatherings, looking for a few people we know, while ignoring new faces that offer opportunities for discipleship and mentoring? In Philippians 2 we read that Christ was the perfect example of humility. He didn't look to his own interests, but to the interests of others (v 4). He did nothing from selfish ambition (v 3). He emptied Himself and became a servant to all (v 5-8, NIV).

Friends, lets follow His example by going into church gatherings looking for new opportunities to love and serve those that we might not yet have a relationship with. Let's be the hands and feet of Jesus by loving unfamiliar faces and making them feel at home. Is it possible that the next discipling relationship you have will not be with someone you know, but with someone you meet for the first time at your next church gathering?

4. Get out of your comfort zone.

We are naturally drawn to comfort as a sailor is drawn to sea. If we aren't careful, we will drown in our own comfort. So how do we negate this constant pull towards comfort and ease? By working hard at doing what *isn't* comfortable. When you walk into a church gathering, seek to move outside of your comfort zone by talking to people you don't know.

- Sit with someone you don't regularly sit by.

- Make sure your conversations with people share the Gospel, not just small talk.

- The point is to intentionally move out of our comfort zones to help others fall in love with God.

14 Thoughts on Mentoring

As someone who has been in full-time ministry for several years, and has been committed to discipleship/mentoring, I've learned a great deal about both. This includes everything from ideas on how you can mentor others to what not to do in the context of a mentoring relationship. I trust that some of these thoughts will be helpful in your pursuit of mentoring for the glory of God!

1. Love people. God uses people who have a great love for others to affect the lives of those surrounding them. Truly love those you mentor.

2. Pray for those you mentor.

3. Be gracious with the people you mentor. Be patient. Mentor with "complete patience and teaching" (2 Timothy 4:2, ESV).

4. God doesn't need you. He chooses to use you to build His kingdom. Always rejoice that He calls you to participate in the work of discipleship/mentoring.

5. Remember that people are always watching you. Imitate Christ. In other words, "practice what you preach." John Newton once said, "People are more likely to be convinced by what they observe of you, than by what they hear from you." Live exemplary lives.

6. Be a source of encouragement to the people you spend time with, not just a source of critcism.

7. Be consistent. The last person people want to spend time with is someone who isn't faithful in meeting together when they say they will.

8. You are not a perfect mentor, so don't try to be.

9. Use your phone. I have found that a spontaneous phone call or text message can go a long way to showing that you care for the people you are mentoring.

10. Ask people the hard questions. It's fine to "bat the breeze" with people, but don't stay there. Be known for asking people the hard questions like, "How are you struggling?" They will be glad you did.

11. Be a good listener. It is a good practice to let others finish their sentence before you begin yours. Listen well. It shows people you care for what they want to share with you.

12. Ask thought-provoking questions. Asking people thought-provoking questions often helps them to realize things about themselves they never would have otherwise. As G.K. Chesterton once said, "It's not that they can't see the solution. They can't see the problem."

13. Reading books together can be a great way to grow with those you mentor.

14. Holding others accountable should be a grace-driven effort. Buck Parsons put it well when he said, "Biblical accountability is first and foremost an arm around the shoulder, not a finger pointing in the face."

Endnotes

1. Mark Dever *Discipling: How to Help Others Follow Jesus* (Wheaton, Illinois: Crossway, 2016) 13.

2. Chuck Lawless, *Making Disciples through Mentoring: Lessons from Paul and Timothy* (Forest, Virginia, and Elkton, Maryland: Church Growth Institute, 2002), 14.

3. Mark Dever often uses the phrase "Doing deliberate spiritual good to help another follow Christ."

4. Phil A. Newton, The Mentoring Church: How Pastors and Congregations Cultivate Leaders. (Kregel Ministry 2017) 34

5. Bruce Shelley, *Church History in Plain Language* (Nashville, Tennessee: Thomas Nelson, 2013), 89.

6. C.J. Mahaney. *Humility* (Colorado Springs, Multnoman 2005) 22.

7. Tony Payne, *How to Walk into Church,* (New South Wales, Matthias Media, 2016), 229.

Notes